EARTH SCIENCE—OUR PLANET **Need to Know**

Plate Tectonics

by D. R. Faust

Consultant: Jordan Stoleru, Science Educator

Minneapolis, Minnesota

Credits

Cover and title page, © VisualProduction/Shutterstock; 3, © desertsolitaire/Adobe Stock; 5, © Vitalii Vitleo/Shutterstock; 7, © Kateryna Kon/Shutterstock; 9, © Naeblys/Shutterstock; 10–11, © DanielFreyr/Adobe Stock; 13, © PeterHermesFurian/iStock; 14–15, © aiisha/Adobe Stock; 17, © Em Campos/Shutterstock; 18, © Peter Hermes Furian/Shutterstock; 19, © antony trivet photography/Shutterstock; 21, © Historic Photo Archive/Getty Images; 22, © The Print Collector/Alamy Stock Photo; 23, © Zaporizhzhia vector/Shutterstock; 25, © Rashevskyi Viacheslav/Shutterstock; 27TL, © Adam Ashburn/Shutterstock; 27TR, © Chen Leopold/Alamy Stock Photo; 27BL, © Florian Nimsdorf/Shutterstock; 27BR, © Andreas Zeitler/Shutterstock; 28, © Designua/Shutterstock.

Bearport Publishing Company Product Development Team

Publisher: Jen Jenson; Director of Product Development: Spencer Brinker; Editorial Director: Allison Juda; Editor: Cole Nelson; Editor: Tiana Tran; Production Editor: Naomi Reich; Art Director: Kim Jones; Designer: Kayla Eggert; Designer: Steve Scheluchin; Production Specialist: Owen Hamlin

Statement on Usage of Generative Artificial Intelligence

Bearport Publishing remains committed to publishing high-quality nonfiction books. Therefore, we restrict the use of generative AI to ensure accuracy of all text and visual components pertaining to a book's subject. See BearportPublishing.com for details.

Library of Congress Cataloging-in-Publication Data

Names: Faust, D. R., author.
Title: Plate tectonics / by D. R. Faust.
Description: Minneapolis, Minnesota : Bearport Publishing Company, [2026] |
   Series: Earth science - our planet : need to know | Includes
   bibliographical references and index.
Identifiers: LCCN 2025001536 (print) | LCCN 2025001537 (ebook) | ISBN
   9798895770702 (library binding) | ISBN 9798895775172 (paperback) | ISBN
   9798895771877 (ebook)
Subjects: LCSH: Plate tectonics–Juvenile literature.
Classification: LCC QE511.4 .F38 2026 (print) | LCC QE511.4 (ebook) | DDC
   551.1/36–dc23/eng/20250212
LC record available at https://lccn.loc.gov/2025001536
LC ebook record available at https://lccn.loc.gov/2025001537

Copyright © 2026 Bearport Publishing Company. All rights reserved. No part of this publication may be reproduced in whole or in part, stored in any retrieval system, or transmitted in any form or by any means, electronic, mechanical, photocopying, recording, or otherwise, without written permission from the publisher. Bearport Publishing is a division of FlutterBee Education Group.

For more information, write to Bearport Publishing, 3500 American Blvd W, Suite 150, Bloomington, MN 55431.

Contents

Puzzle It Out 4

Looking Inside 6

Under Your Feet 8

Large and Small. 12

Always Moving. 14

Together and Apart. 16

Shake It Up!. 20

It All Fits 22

Things to Come. 26

Shaping the Land 28

SilverTips for Success 29

Glossary .30

Read More 31

Learn More Online 31

Index 32

About the Author. 32

Puzzle It Out

The pieces of a jigsaw puzzle fit together perfectly. Their edges all line up. Earth's surface is a lot like a big jigsaw. It has huge, moving slabs of rock covering it. The **theory** that the planet has moving pieces on its surface is called plate tectonics (tek-TAH-niks).

Geologists are scientists who study Earth. They look at the rocks the planet is made of. Often, they can learn about Earth's history this way. Some geologists study plate tectonics.

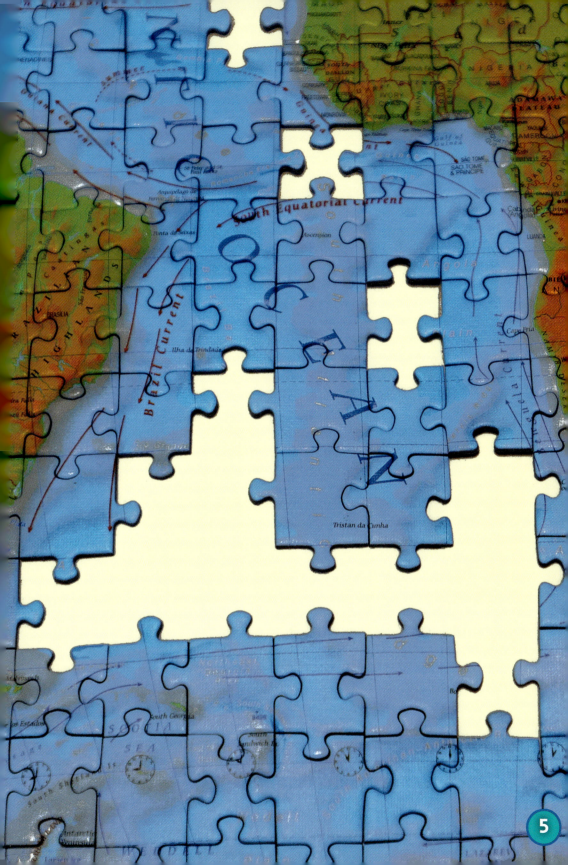

Looking Inside

Earth is made up of several layers. Each one is a little bit different. The top layer is called the **crust**. Under the crust is the **mantle**. The very center of Earth is called the core. This part has two layers. There is an inner and outer core.

Earth's inner core is a solid chunk of metal. The outer core is wrapped around that. It is made of liquid metal.

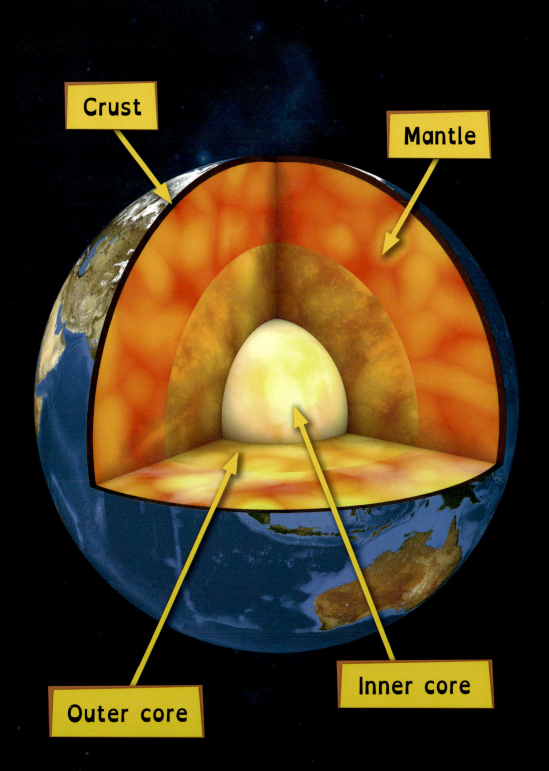

Under Your Feet

Earth's crust is like an outer shell. It is made of thick rock. All the land and water are found on this layer of Earth. But the crust is not a single piece of rock. It is broken up into huge slabs called tectonic plates.

There are many things living on Earth's crust. But as far as we know there is no life below the crust. The mantle and core are too hot for living things to survive.

Tectonic plates divide Earth's crust into sections.

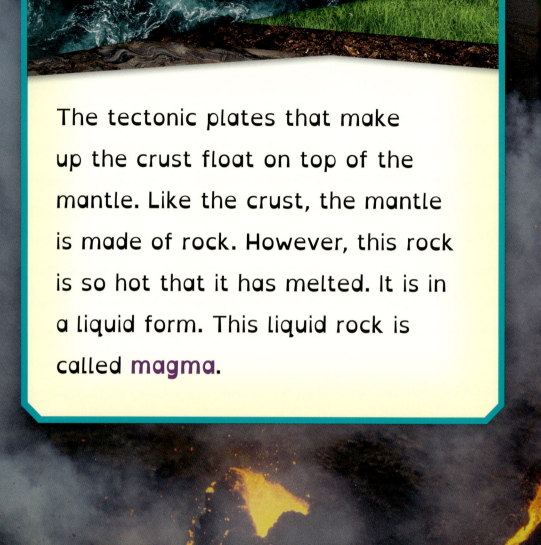

The tectonic plates that make up the crust float on top of the mantle. Like the crust, the mantle is made of rock. However, this rock is so hot that it has melted. It is in a liquid form. This liquid rock is called **magma**.

Sometimes, magma pushes up out of the mantle. It breaks through the crust to the surface. When this happens, the liquid rock is called lava.

Lava

Large and Small

There are about 15 tectonic plates of different sizes. These include seven larger major plates. There are also about eight smaller minor plates. The major plates mostly align with Earth's land. Many of them line up with the seven **continents**. The largest major plate goes around the Pacific Ocean.

There are different kinds of plates below land and water. The ones below land are thick and very old. Plates below the ocean are thinner.

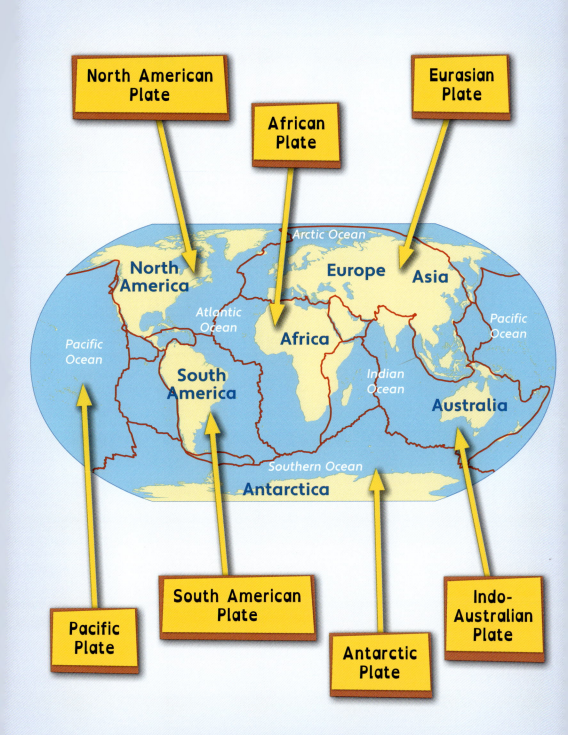

Always Moving

Because they are floating on the liquid mantle, tectonic plates are always moving. We just don't feel the shifting because it is so slow. The plates take a very long time to move even a small distance. Still, this movement has a huge impact on the world.

Tectonic plates move only about 1 to 2 inches (2.5 to 5 cm) each year. That is about the same speed a fingernail grows.

Slow plate movement below our feet shapes what we see all around.

Together and Apart

Some tectonic plates are moving toward each other. When two plates come together, the land at the edges can get pushed up. It can fold and crumple. Over millions of years, the land is often built up higher and higher. This can form mountains.

The Himalayas is a mountain range in Asia. It can be found where the Eurasian Plate and the Indo-Australian Plate meet. The plates crashed together more than 40 million years ago.

Some plates move away from each other. The land at the edges falls as the plates slide apart. This can form a **rift**, or a large crack. Sometimes, magma from the mantle pushes up through these cracks. When this hot rock cools, it makes new **landforms**.

When magma pushes through the crust, it creates a volcano. There are a lot of volcanoes around the edges of the Pacific Plate. This area is sometimes called the Ring of Fire.

Asia

North America

Pacific Ocean

Atlantic Ocean

Ring of Fire

Indian Ocean

South America

Australia

The Great Rift Valley runs from the Middle East to southeastern Africa.

Shake It Up!

When two plates meet, they can rub and get stuck. **Pressure** builds up. As the plates finally slide apart, the pressure is released. This often causes the ground to shake. We feel the movement as earthquakes. When this happens under water, it can set off big waves called tsunamis (tsu-NAH-meez).

The edge where two plates meet is called a **fault**. Earthquakes and volcanoes are common along faults. These places often have mountains or rifts, too.

San Francisco, California, was hit by a huge earthquake in 1906.

It All Fits

Earth is about 4.5 billion years old. Over time, its surface has changed a lot. The movement of tectonic plates has caused the continents to move, too. They have shifted slowly over a long period of time. This process is called **continental drift**.

In 1912, scientist Alfred Wegener came up with the idea that the continents move over time. But the theory was mostly ignored by scientists until the 1950s.

Continental Drift

225 million years ago

150 million years ago

65 million years ago

Present day

At the beginning of the time of the dinosaurs, the continents were together. They formed a single **supercontinent**. Scientists call it Pangea (pan-JEE-uh). Over time, the tectonic plates continued to move. It took millions of years for the continents to shift to where they are today.

Geologists think Africa is splitting apart. As the plates move, a large rift in east Africa grows. In a few million years, a new ocean could form there. It might separate Africa into two continents.

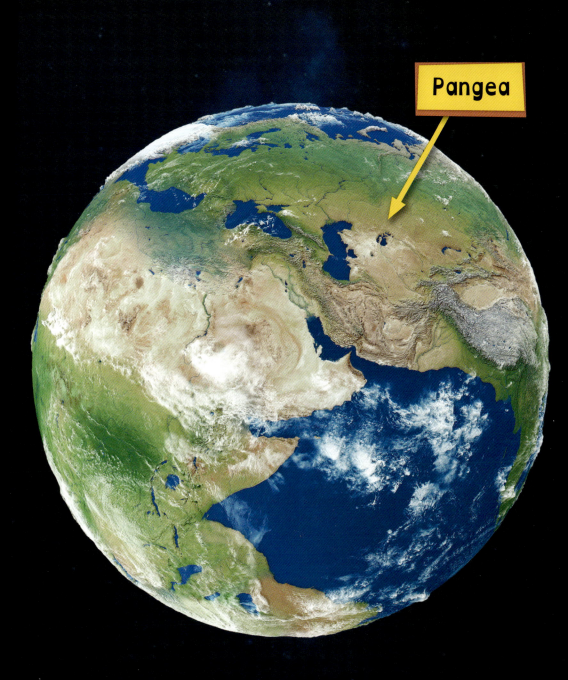

Things to Come

Earth's tectonic plates have long shaped the planet. And they will continue to do so. Their movement will create mountains and rifts. Earthquakes and volcanoes will also change the surface. And continental drift will reshape entire continents. It all comes down to plate tectonics.

In the next 250 million years, continental drift will likely create another supercontinent. The Pacific Ocean may disappear. And the Atlantic Ocean could get much bigger. This would bring all the land together.

Shaping the Land

As tectonic plates shift and move over time, they change the land. They can form mountains and rifts.

Two plates pushing against each other can make the land crumple and push up.

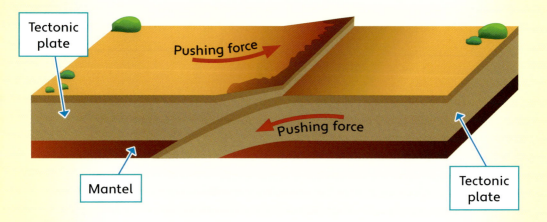

Two plates can pull apart. The land on top of the plates shifts as well. Sometimes, this leads to volcanoes. Often, it forms rifts.

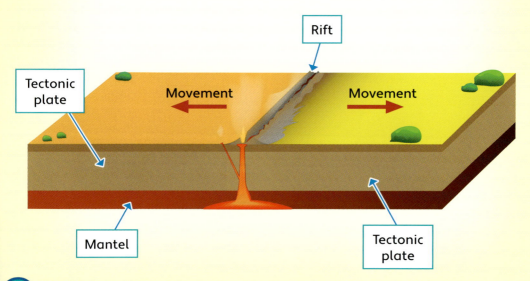

SilverTips for SUCCESS

★ SilverTips for REVIEW

Review what you've learned. Use the text to help you.

Define key terms

crust
magma
mantle
rift
tectonic plates

Check for understanding

What are the different layers of Earth?

Describe how one kind of landform is created by the movement of tectonic plates.

What is continental drift, and how does it help shape the surface of Earth?

Think deeper

Earth's surface is always changing. Consider how your life would be different if plate tectonics changed the land near where you live.

★ SilverTips on TEST-TAKING

- **Make a study plan.** Ask your teacher what the test is going to cover. Then, set aside time to study a little bit every day.

- **Read all the questions carefully.** Be sure you know what is being asked.

- **Skip any questions** you don't know how to answer right away. Mark them and come back later if you have time.

Glossary

continental drift the slow movement of the continents on Earth's mantle

continents the seven large land masses on Earth

crust Earth's hard outer layer

fault the edges where two tectonic plates meet

landforms natural features on Earth's surface

magma hot liquid rock beneath the surface of Earth

mantle the layer inside Earth just below the crust where magma flows

pressure the force made by pressing on something

rift a deep crack or opening in the ground

supercontinent a former large continent that is assumed to have existed and from which other continents broke off and drifted away

theory an idea that explains something

Read More

Earley, Christina. *Plate Tectonics (Earth and Space Science).* Coral Springs, FL: Seahorse Publishing, 2023.

Kuehl, Ashley. *Mountains and Cliffs (Earth Science–Landforms: Need to Know).* Minneapolis: Bearport Publishing Company, 2025.

Nixon, Madeline. *Earthquakes (Natural Disasters).* Minneapolis: Kaleidoscope, 2023.

Learn More Online

1. Go to **FactSurfer.com** or scan the QR code below.

2. Enter "**Plate Tectonics**" into the search box.

3. Click on the cover of this book to see a list of websites.

Index

continental 22–23, 26

core 6–8

crust 6–8, 10–11, 18

earthquakes 20–21, 26

lava 11

magma 10–11, 18

mantle 6–8, 10–11, 14, 18

mountains 16, 20, 26, 28

plate movement 14, 20, 22, 26, 28

plate tectonics 4, 26

rifts 18–20, 24, 26, 28

rock 4, 8, 10–11, 18

supercontinent 24, 26

tectonic plates 8–10, 12, 14, 16, 22, 24, 26, 28

volcanoes 18, 20, 26, 28

About the Author

D. R. Faust is a freelance writer of fiction and nonfiction. They live in Queens, NY.